Original title:
The Winter Woods

Author: Kene Elistrand
ISBN HARDBACK: 978-9908-52-008-7
ISBN PAPERBACK: 978-9908-52-009-4
ISBN EBOOK: 978-9908-52-010-0

Glimmers of Light in Frozen Corners

In shadows deep, the whispers play,
A flicker glows, then fades away.
Frozen edges, secrets hold,
Glimmers of light, soft tales unfold.

The icy breath upon the stone,
In stillness, warmth can be known.
Through crystal veils, the dawn breaks free,
Tender hues, a silent plea.

Wanderings in a Silvered Landscape

Footprints trace the silver ground,
Where dreams and echoes can be found.
Whispering winds through silent trees,
In winter's grasp, a gentle breeze.

A world transformed, so stark, so wide,
With glistening paths that softly guide.
Here, lost thoughts begin to swell,
In every flake, a tale to tell.

The Yearning of Bare Branches

Bare branches stretch against the sky,
In quietude, they wait and sigh.
Their dreams are woven with the breeze,
A longing song beneath the freeze.

Each empty limb a story holds,
Of whispered winds and winter's folds.
Through frosty nights, they softly ache,
In search of spring, their hearts awake.

When Dusk Descends on the Frost

As dusk descends, the chill does creep,
In twilight's grasp, the world falls asleep.
Soft shadows dance on fields of white,
A hush descends, enveloped in night.

The stars emerge with twinkling light,
A silent watch through frigid night.
When dreams take flight in frosty air,
The heart finds peace, a stillness rare.

Constellations in the Snowfall

Glistening flakes drift down from the sky,
They twinkle like stars, so light as they fly.
Each one a wish, a dream that we hold,
With whispers of winter, a story unfolds.

The world turns to magic, a silent delight,
In silence we wander, through shimmer and light.
A blanket of wonders, so fragile, so bright,
Constellations of snow, painting the night.

Blankets of Stillness

A hush wraps the earth in gentle embrace,
Snow pillows the ground, a soft, tender space.
Time seems to pause in this wintery realm,
Blankets of stillness at nature's helm.

Footprints are muffled, like secrets we keep,
Under the blanket, the world falls asleep.
Every breath taken, a cloud in the air,
In blankets of stillness, we find peace to share.

Shadows Cast on a Frozen Canvas

The sun dips low, as daylight may fade,
Shadows stretch long on the white masquerade.
Each tree a silhouette, bold and serene,
Canvas of frost, where beauty is seen.

The twilight paints stories, in colors so cold,
In whispers of twilight, our memories told.
Frozen impressions that time can't erase,
Shadows dance lightly on winter's soft face.

Hushed Footfalls in the Chill

With each careful step through a world cloaked in white,
Hushed footfalls echo, in the quiet of night.
Breath misting softly in the cold, crisp air,
Every step speaks softly, our secrets laid bare.

The chill wraps around us, a shiver of grace,
In moments of stillness, we find our own place.
Together we wander, in shadows and light,
Hushed footfalls leading, with wonder in sight.

Enchanted Nights of Frosted Stars

In the silence of the night,
Stars shimmer with frozen light.
Whispers float on icy air,
Dreams awaken without a care.

Trees adorned in silver lace,
Nature's beauty, a timeless grace.
Underneath the glowing sky,
Wishes dance and softly lie.

A gentle breeze begins to weave,
Magic threads we dare believe.
Each flake tells a tale untold,
Winter's jewel, a sight to behold.

Crystals gather, pure and bright,
Guardians of this tranquil night.
Moments paused in frosty time,
Echoes of a whispered rhyme.

In this realm where shadows play,
Enchanted nights shall never stray.
Underneath the cosmos' dome,
Frosted stars, forever home.

Breaths of Winter’s Magic

In the air, a chilling sigh,
Winter's breath, a soft goodbye.
Nature wraps in blankets white,
A world transformed, pure and bright.

Frosty patterns on the glass,
Time stands still as moments pass.
With every step, the crunch below,
Echoes of the season's glow.

Silvery trees, silent and tall,
Brimming with secrets, they enthrall.
As daylight fades, shadows blend,
In this magic, time suspends.

Warm hearts gather, stories shared,
In this cold, we find we cared.
With laughter ringing through the air,
Winter's charm, beyond compare.

A tapestry of dreams aligned,
Breaths of winter, intertwined.
In frozen beauty, spirits soar,
Magic lingers, always more.

Beneath a Veil of Sparkling Ice

Underneath the frost-kissed glow,
A world is wrapped in white below.
Whispers travel through the night,
Magic glimmers, pure delight.

Branches wear a crystal crown,
Nature's splendor, handed down.
Each breath mingles with the cold,
Stories of the brave and bold.

In the stillness, shadows play,
Dancing softly, night and day.
Winter's song, a gentle strain,
Soothing echoes in the lane.

A shiver runs through every tree,
Life holds on with tender glee.
Beneath the veil, there's warmth inside,
In frozen silence, hearts confide.

Sparkling dreams like stars above,
In this world, we learn to love.
Beneath the glow of winter's might,
Pure serenity in the night.

The Spirit of a Frosty Dawn

As dawn breaks with frosty breath,
Whispers of silence chase away death.
Colors dance in morning's light,
Pure and bright, a joyful sight.

Chill in the air yet warmth within,
A promise carries, fresh to begin.
Nature shivers, stretching wide,
Welcoming the day, arms open wide.

Misty tendrils weave their way,
In harmony, the world shall play.
Every leaf, a twinkling gem,
In the morn, we all condemn.

Golden rays through icy haze,
Guiding dreams in frosty maze.
Step by step, we find our song,
In the spirit where we belong.

With each breath, a lilting sound,
Life awakens, peace is found.
The frosty dawn, a tale retold,
In winter's heart, we find our gold.

The Stillness of Nature’s Breath

In the dawn's gentle light,
Whispers stir through the trees,
Softly nature calls forth,
A symphony on the breeze.

Leaves rustle with secrets,
As shadows dance on the ground,
A stillness wraps the world,
In beauty, peace is found.

The brook hums a quiet tune,
While clouds drift lazily by,
The sun stretches its rays,
Painting gold across the sky.

Mountains stand strong and tall,
Guardians of tranquil grace,
Each moment here is life,
In nature's warm embrace.

Here time seems to stand still,
As magic fills the air,
In the stillness of nature,
All worries disappear.

Crystals on the Forest Floor

Glistening in the sunlight,
Each drop a fleeting star,
Crystals dot the forest floor,
A treasure near and far.

Amongst the mossy shadows,
They shimmer with delight,
Reflecting nature's wonders,
In the calm, morning light.

Footsteps whisper softly,
As deer tread lightly through,
A world adorned in splendor,
In every sparkling hue.

Leaves drop like gentle rain,
Cascading from the trees,
Each crystal holds a story,
Carried by the breeze.

Nature's art in silence,
Forever will it be,
A dance of light and shadows,
In the woods, wild and free.

Frost-kissed Memories

In the quiet of winter's breath,
Frost paints the world anew,
Each flake a soft reminder,
Of memories once held true.

The meadow, cloaked in silence,
Hides whispers of the past,
A blanket of frost-kissed dreams,
In a beauty unsurpassed.

Footsteps crunching on the snow,
Leaves tales of times gone by,
Each moment, crisp and fleeting,
Underneath the pale sky.

The chill wraps ‘round like velvet,
As stars begin to glow,
Frost-kissed, the night whispers,
Of love and warmth below.

In the depth of winter's heart,
Lies a promise of the spring,
For each frost-kissed memory,
A song of hope to sing.

Paths Woven in White

Winding trails through the woods,
Dressed in a cloak of snow,
Each path is a journey shared,
With stories yet to show.

Footprints trace the silence,
Leading to places unseen,
In a world of white wonder,
Where magic reigns supreme.

Trees stand like sentinels high,
With branches draped in lace,
A winter's breath caresses,
This peaceful, sacred space.

The sun plays hide and seek,
While shadows softly blend,
Paths woven in pure white,
Invite each heart to mend.

In the stillness of the snow,
We find our compass true,
Paths woven in white reveal,
The beauty straight and new.

Serenity in Subzero Silence

In the stillness of the night,
Snow blankets the earth, pure and white.
Stars twinkle above in a vast expanse,
Whispers of winter invite a trance.

Silent shadows drift and sway,
Chilling breezes softly play.
The world hushed under frost's embrace,
Finding peace in this quiet space.

Each breath clouds in the air,
Frozen moments linger, rare.
A tranquil heart beats slow and low,
In subzero silence, time moves slow.

Frosty branches gently cling,
Nature rests as nightbirds sing.
Layers of ice like mirrors gleam,
In this solitude, we dream.

Calm descends, a sacred balm,
Winter's touch, a soothing psalm.
Here in this pristine, peaceful scene,
Serenity reigns, beautifully keen.

The Charm of Twinkling Snowflakes

Delicate dancers, graceful and light,
Snowflakes twirling in the soft moonlight.
Each one unique, a masterpiece rare,
They whisper secrets, floating in air.

Gentle winds carry their drift,
Nature's wonders, the most precious gift.
A canvas of white, a frosty ballet,
Enchanting the night, driving cares away.

Children laugh in snowy play,
Building dreams with every sway.
Winter's charm wrapped in cold's embrace,
Twinkling snowflakes, a warming grace.

They sparkle like jewels, shine on the ground,
In the heart of winter, beauty is found.
A soft touch here, a kiss up high,
In this twinkling dance, spirits fly.

With each flake that lands, a story unfolds,
Of magical winters, of warmth never cold.
The charm of nature, a sight to adore,
In the dance of snowflakes, we seek to explore.

The Quietude of Shimmering Pines

In a forest where the tall pines stand,
Whispers of winter grace the land.
Branches heavy with snow, pristine white,
Shimmering softly in the moon's light.

Beneath a blanket, the earth is still,
Nature rests, embraced by chill.
Birds have settled, hushed their tunes,
While stars blink over the darkened dunes.

A tranquil path through frosted trees,
Carried gently on the whispering breeze.
Memories linger in the frosty air,
In the quietude, we find care.

The scent of pine, fresh and true,
Guides our spirits, a soft avenue.
With every step, the silence sings,
Wrapped in the warmth that winter brings.

A moment savored, peace defined,
In shimmering pines, our souls unwind.
Nature's embrace, a calming delight,
In this winter haven, hearts take flight.

Nature’s Frozen Reverie

In the heart of winter's grasp,
Nature holds us in a gentle clasp.
Mountains wear a crown of snow,
A frozen reverie, soft and slow.

Rivers whisper under icy coats,
Dreaming of spring on invisible boats.
Time stands still in this silent show,
As dreams weave through the fallen glow.

A world transformed, serene and bright,
Giving birth to thoughts of light.
Each flake a wish, a whispered plea,
Forever cherished in memory.

Life holds its breath beneath the white,
Amidst the hush, we find delight.
In muted tones, the landscape sighs,
Nature’s frozen beauty never lies.

As nights turn long and days grow short,
In winter’s arms, find your support.
For in this reverie, solace found,
In nature’s chorus, love resounds.

The Enchantment of Silent Branches

In winter's grasp, the branches sway,
Whispers of frost in soft array.
Beneath the moon, a silver light,
Silent magic, pure and bright.

Nature holds its breath so deep,
Dreams awaken from their sleep.
Each flake dances, soft and slow,
In this realm, where time won't flow.

The trees wear coats of icy lace,
A stillness wraps this hallowed space.
In shadows faint, the secrets gleam,
Cradled softly, like a dream.

The stars above begin to twinkle,
As nature's heart begins to crinkle.
In the calm, the world feels wide,
Enchantment waits, our hearts as guide.

Lullaby of the Frozen Earth

Beneath the sky of pale cerulean,
The earth lies still, a frozen union.
In whispers low, the winds do sing,
A lullaby on softest wing.

Glistening fields wrap in their dreams,
Crystals shine as the moonlight beams.
Nature's hush, a soothing balm,
Every breath is soft and calm.

The trees in silence, watching near,
Guard our dreams, embrace our fear.
In stillness found, we drift away,
As night embraces closing day.

Frosty breath fills the air around,
In this moment, peace is found.
Wrapped in layers, warm, and tight,
Whispers of love fill the night.

Frosty Veils and Shimmering Dreams

A veil of frost cloaks every sight,
Underneath the stars so bright.
Whispers from the frosty ground,
Weaving dreams that swirl around.

The night enfolds with diamond light,
In shadows deep, the world feels right.
Veils of winter softly glide,
Through the magic, we confide.

The crickets hush, the owls take flight,
In the warmth of the starry night.
Each breath a cloud of silken white,
In this fleeting, wondrous sight.

With every heartbeat, dreams awake,
In frosty realms, our cares forsake.
Beyond the chill, a love ignites,
Within the cold, our hearts take flight.

A Haven of White Silence

In the still of winter’s embrace,
A haven found, a sacred space.
White silence drapes the world so wide,
In this calm, our hearts abide.

Softly falls the blanket pure,
Each flake a promise, fresh and sure.
Among the trees, a gentle sigh,
As dreams unfold beneath the sky.

The quiet speaks in glistening tones,
A path is carved, where no one roams.
Every step leaves prints of grace,
In the snow, a tranquil place.

Here time stands still, the world asleep,
In our hearts, the memories keep.
Wrapped in white, the silence reigns,
A haven where peace forever remains.

Whispers of the Woodland Spirits

In the hush of emerald trees,
Soft voices drift on the breeze.
Secrets wrapped in mossy shrouds,
Nature sings beneath the crowds.

Moonlit paths with shadows dance,
Glimmers caught in a furtive glance.
Echoes of the past resound,
In every leaf that's gently found.

Murmurs weave through twinkling lights,
Guiding souls on tranquil nights.
The forest breathes with ancient lore,
As whispers call from the woodland floor.

Crisp air tinged with earthy dew,
Awakens dreams, both strange and true.
Each rustle holds a fleeting tale,
Of life that stirs beneath the veil.

Here, where gentle spirits play,
In twilight's glow, they find their way.
A symphony of peace unfolds,
In whispers soft, the forest molds.

Footprints of a Frigid Soul

In the silence of winter's grip,
Frosty trails on an icy slip.
Shadows linger in the chill,
Echoes of a heart stood still.

Snowflakes dance like whispers pale,
Each one tells a lonely tale.
Beneath the stars, the world feels tight,
Wrapped in dark, away from light.

Bare branches stretch towards the sky,
In the stillness, memories sigh.
Footprints mark the frozen ground,
Traces of lost words unbound.

A cold breeze carries soft lament,
From a soul that’s weary, spent.
Yet in this frosted solitude,
There’s a hint of strength renewed.

In every breath, a spark may flame,
Resilient warmth amidst the pain.
Though winter wraps its icy shroud,
Hope still whispers, soft but loud.

The Dance of the Frosted Leaves

In autumn’s breath, the leaves take flight,
Dancing softly in fading light.
A symphony of colors bright,
Swirling dreams in crisp delight.

Frosted edges glinting clear,
Nature’s beauty, drawing near.
With every swirl, a story told,
Of summer sun and winter’s cold.

Breezes carry laughter's tune,
Beneath the watchful harvest moon.
Each leaf a note in nature’s song,
Together they spin where they belong.

Amidst the chaos, grace prevails,
Guided by the autumn gales.
From tree to ground, a gentle sweep,
In this dance, the world’s asleep.

As twilight drapes its silken shroud,
Leaves embrace the night, so loud.
In their rhythm, whispers weave,
The dance of life, we all believe.

Twilight's Embrace of Silence

As daylight fades, the shadows play,
Twilight wraps the world in gray.
A lullaby in hues of blue,
Softly calls the night anew.

Stars emerge, their gentle light,
Guiding dreams into the night.
Whispers echo through the dusk,
In the stillness, a calming husk.

Soft silhouettes of trees stand tall,
Guarding secrets, they hear it all.
Silence dances in muted tones,
Welcoming the night’s hushed moans.

The moon hangs low, a silver gleam,
Bathing all in its tender beam.
In this embrace, we find retreat,
As the heart slows to its beat.

In twilight’s hold, a serene grace,
Life finds peace in the vast space.
In every breath, the world ignites,
With whispers soft, in starry nights.

Branches Draped in White

Beneath the weight of winter's grace,
Branches draped in white embrace.
Whispers of silence fill the air,
As snowflakes drift without a care.

In twilight's glow, a soft descent,
The world transformed, a pure event.
Each crystal spark, a tale untold,
In nature's arms, the night unfolds.

The moonlight bathes the frozen scene,
A canvas bright, in shades of cream.
While shadows dance on frosted ground,
A symphony of beauty found.

Cold breezes hum a gentle tune,
As stars emerge, a silver boon.
In tranquil moments, hearts take flight,
Among the branches draped in white.

Twilight in the Enchanted Thicket

Amidst the trees where whispers lie,
Twilight drapes a dusky sky.
A gentle breeze begins to weave,
Secrets that the shadows leave.

Petals fall like dreams unleashed,
Colors fade, the day has ceased.
Silhouettes in twilight glow,
Guide the path where fairies go.

Luminous eyes peer from the dark,
Creating magic with each spark.
The thicket whispers soft and low,
Tales of wonder from long ago.

With every step, enchantment calls,
In hidden realms where twilight falls.
A dance of dusk, a fleeting sigh,
In the thicket where dreams fly.

Secrets of the Snow-Capped Glade

In the glade where secrets keep,
Snow-capped whispers softly sleep.
Where every flake, a story spun,
Of battles lost and victories won.

Mighty pines stand tall and proud,
Guarding dreams beneath the shroud.
Footprints lead through frosty air,
A journey rich with silent care.

Veiled in mist, the echoes wake,
Of laughter shared, of hearts that ache.
In every corner, magic weaves,
Tales of old that nature leaves.

Windsong carries secrets far,
Underneath the evening star.
While the glade, in tranquil peace,
Holds memories that never cease.

The Dance of Shivering Shadows

In moonlit nights, where shadows play,
A dance begins, the night holds sway.
Whispers twine in the cool night air,
Where every movement speaks of care.

Beneath the boughs, the figures weave,
A tale of light, e'er hard to believe.
The flick'ring fireflies join the jest,
As shadows sway, they are blessed.

Through dim-lit glades, the spirits glide,
With every step, enchantment bides.
A harmony of dark and light,
In the dance of shadows, pure delight.

In every twist, a secret spun,
Until the dawn reveals the fun.
The dance concludes, yet whispers stay,
Of shivering shadows that fade away.

Shadows Cast by a Pale Sun

Beneath the waning light we tread,
Whispers of dusk paint all in grey.
Shadows stretch, their secrets spread,
As silence drapes the world in sway.

A fleeting breeze, a ghostly sigh,
Threads of memory weave through time.
In twilight's grasp we softly lie,
Where echoes linger, deep and prime.

Glimmers fade with each heartbeat's pause,
Nature's canvas, soft and bare.
The day concedes to night's applause,
In shadows cast, we find our care.

Fleeting glances, moments lost,
In the dusk, we find our place.
The pale sun melts, the line is crossed,
As dreams and shadows interlace.

Let us linger, hearts aglow,
In the dusk's embrace, we stand.
Time flows gently, like the snow,
In shadows cast by a pale hand.

The Allure of Crystal Canopies

Through branches intertwined we roam,
A world adorned in diamond light.
Beneath the trees, we build our home,
Where whispers dance in soft twilight.

Leaves of glass reflect our gaze,
A shimmering path of dreams untold.
In nature's maze, we lose our ways,
As time within the silence unfolds.

Iridescent hues take flight,
Colors gleam with every breath.
In the heart of day and night,
The crystal whispers life and death.

Each spark a wish, each glimmer fate,
A tapestry of shadows sways.
In this embrace, we resonate,
Finding magic in earthly ways.

Cradled by the whispered breeze,
Underneath the vibrant show.
In crystal canopies with ease,
We find the solace interwoven slow.

Winter’s Gentle Caress

In the stillness of the night,
Snowflakes dance on frosty air.
Wrapped in warmth, beneath the light,
Winter holds us in her care.

Every breath a silver dream,
Crystals twinkle on each tree.
Nature dressed in purest gleam,
A silent song, her harmony.

Footsteps trace a path so bright,
Every echo soft and clear.
Whispers carried through the night,
In this world, we have no fear.

Winter’s breath, a soothing balm,
Cocooned in white, we rest and wait.
Wrapped in peace, our hearts feel calm,
While the world outside stands straight.

Let us cherish this embrace,
As the cold winds start to play.
In winter’s gentle, softest chase,
We find warmth in every sway.

Secrets Breathed by Bare Trees

In quiet woods, the secrets sleep,
Bare branches stretch towards the sky.
Nature whispers, secrets deep,
As winds of change begin to sigh.

Nonchalant, the leaves have fled,
Exposing tales of days gone by.
In every twist, a history said,
With every breeze, the spirits fly.

Roots entwined in earth's embrace,
Guardians of stories old and wise.
In shadows cast, we find our place,
While silent echoes serenely rise.

Time stands still beneath their care,
Each hollow trunk, a ghostly friend.
In every sigh, a whispered prayer,
As memories of life transcend.

Underneath the moonlit dome,
The bare trees share their ancient lore.
In nature's heart, we find our home,
Where secrets breathe forevermore.

Starlit Whispers

In the night where secrets dwell,
Softly shine the stars that tell.
Whispers ride the gentle breeze,
Carrying dreams from ancient trees.

Moonlight dances on the ground,
Echoes of a hush profound.
Every twinkle sparks a wish,
In the silence, hearts will swish.

Beneath the vast celestial dome,
Rest so many tales of home.
In the calm, time seems to pause,
Nature's beauty gently claws.

Sighing softly, shadows weave,
Magic finds us when we believe.
Through the dark, a path is lit,
In starlit whispers, hope will sit.

Forever, under starry night's glow,
We find the peace the heart can know.
Whispers linger, sweet and bright,
Guiding souls through endless night.

Winter’s Breath, A Tale of Ice and Whispered Promises

Winter breathes a chilling sigh,
Silent flakes begin to fly.
Each one holds a promise true,
A story told in glimmering hue.

Trees wear coats of sparkling white,
Blankets fold in soft moonlight.
In the stillness, time stands still,
Nature whispers, bends to will.

Frosty patterns on the glass,
Reflect the hours that quietly pass.
Underneath the icy veneer,
Lies a heart that beats sincere.

With every crack, a tale unfolds,
Of warmth and dreams, of hopes untold.
In the heart of winter's wane,
Life awakens, breaking chain.

Above, a canvas gray and pale,
Holds the hints of spring's sweet trail.
In the frost, a life renews,
Whispered promises in soft hues.

Winter’s Walk through Enchanted Ferns

Upon a path where ferns reside,
The snowflakes fall, a quiet glide.
Whispers swirl in frosted air,
As nature dons her wintry wear.

Winding trails and hidden nooks,
Beneath the snow, the forest cooks.
Silent echoes, timeless grace,
In this land, we find our place.

Every footstep crunches neat,
In dreamlike dance, our hearts will meet.
Among the ferns, so soft, so green,
Lies the magic, barely seen.

Through the branches, sunlight peeps,
Awakening the world that sleeps.
Nature's charm wraps us both tight,
In winter's walk, hearts burn bright.

Here we linger, hand in hand,
In a world so tender and grand.
Through enchanted ferns we roam,
Together, we find our way home.

The Hidden Life Beneath the Frost

Beneath the frost, life stirs and breathes,
In whispers soft, the quiet weaves.
Roots run deep through frozen ground,
In secret dreams, new hopes are found.

Each blade of grass, dormant yet bold,
Holds stories waiting to be told.
In the silence, life awaits,
As winter's veil contemplates.

Icicles glitter, crystals sway,
Hints of warmth in the light of day.
An ancient pulse, a rhythmic beat,
The hidden life beneath, discreet.

From the chill, a promise grows,
The world pauses, yet still flows.
Awakening from slumber, souls ignite,
In the dance of day and night.

So when you tread on snowy trails,
Remember where the whispers hail.
Beyond the frost, beneath the light,
Life’s hidden wonders take their flight.

Lurking Beneath the Frozen Boughs

In the silence deep and still,
Creatures shimmer with winter's chill.
Beneath the frost, they lie in wait,
For spring's bright dawn, a new fate.

Shadows dance, whispers merge,
Nature holds a quiet urge.
Leaves of ice on branches cling,
In dreams of warmth, the forest sings.

The frozen lake holds secrets tight,
Reflections caught in pale moonlight.
Roots entwined in snow’s cold grasp,
Nature holds its breath, a gasp.

A hidden world beneath the frost,
Unseen lives, paths crossed and lost.
Veils of white that softly veil,
Echoes of an age-old tale.

Yet hope lies deep in frozen ground,
Where life will rise, profound, unbound.
Beneath the boughs, a promise stirs,
Awakening hearts, as winter blurs.

Pines and Shadows Under a Glistening Blanket

Snowflakes fall, a gentle hush,
Pines stand tall in winter's crush.
Shadows stretch beneath their height,
Whispers caught in soft moonlight.

Glistening blankets cover all,
Nature's hush, a gentle thrall.
Each branch, heavy with icy dreams,
In stillness, a world redeems.

Footsteps crunch on frozen ground,
Echoes lost, lost yet found.
Nature’s coat in purest white,
Holds mysteries of the night.

Sky alight with stars that gleam,
Dancing softly, a tranquil dream.
Pines embrace the cold so deep,
In silence, secrets softly sleep.

Underneath this frozen dome,
Life awaits, a quiet home.
The glistening blanket, smooth and wide,
Holds the beauty that we must hide.

Haikus of Hibernation

Beneath blankets tight,
Whispers of dreams softly weave,
Nature sways in sleep.

Silent breaths echo,
Warmth encased in the frost's grip,
Time still, shadows blend.

Furry hearts nestled,
Winter's embrace shields them close,
Hidden from the storm.

Cold winds gently blow,
Nature hums a lullaby,
Branches bow and sigh.

In quiet repose,
Each moment drifts like soft snow,
Spring waits in the hush.

Conversations in the Cold

Frosty whispers drift near,
Breezes murmur, crisp and clear.
Trees converse in ancient tongue,
Words of winter softly sung.

Footsteps crunch on frozen earth,
Nature shares her tales of birth.
Life, though still, will find a way,
In the chill of winter’s stay.

Under stars, stories unfold,
Of warmth and courage bold.
Branches sway in soft ballet,
Dancing to the night’s display.

Silent moments, hearts attune,
Stars blink softly, a silent tune.
Every glance, a cherished thread,
Woven in winter’s quiet bed.

As frost adorns each bough,
Nature listens, here and now.
In the cold, a bond takes hold,
Stories told, folk tales of old.

Silence of the Frozen Haven

In winter's grasp, the stillness reigns,
Whispers of snow dance down the lanes.
Trees wear coats of icy white,
Underneath, the world feels right.

Footsteps lost in softest fleece,
Nature's hush brings timeless peace.
Crystal orbs hang, pure and bright,
A tapestry of silvery light.

Each breath forms a cloud in air,
Moments linger, devoid of care.
Frozen lakes like mirrors shine,
Reflecting dreams in winter's design.

Amidst this chill, hearts gather near,
In the silence, warmth appears.
Wrapped in layers, souls connect,
In frozen mere, we find respect.

So let this haven heal and mend,
With every snowflake, love descends.
In silence deep, we find our place,
A frozen haven, full of grace.

The Heartbeat of an Arctic Suburb

In the quiet streets, life unfolds,
With hidden stories, quietly told.
Under the glow of a pale streetlamp,
An anchoring pulse, a vibrant stamp.

Snowflakes fall like gentle sighs,
From winter's breath, the city lies.
Children laugh and boots crunch snow,
A warmth in hearts, a glowing show.

Neighbors gather, sharing tales,
Through frosted windows, spirit sails.
The heartbeat thumps, a steady thrum,
In Arctic nights, good times come.

Amidst the chill, a fire ignites,
Bringing together the coldest nights.
Each echoed laugh a pulse so true,
In every heart, winter's hue.

As the stars twinkle above so bright,
Their glimmer feels like hope and light.
In this suburb, we find our song,
Through icy paths, we all belong.

Dreams Adrift in the Coldsnap

In whispers low, dreams take their flight,
Across the canvas of endless night.
Frosted windows frame visions grand,
While shadows play, soft as sand.

Each flake a wish, drifting down,
In the silent cool of a snow-laden town.
Hopes intertwine in the crystal glow,
Lifting spirits, as the cold winds blow.

An echoing chime in the frozen air,
A melody of dreams laid bare.
In every heart, a flicker gleams,
As we wander through winter's dreams.

Beneath the frost, we find our muse,
The chill ignites what we choose.
In the depth of night, we boldly roam,
While dreams find warmth, they journey home.

So let the coldsnap inspire our thought,
As beauty in silence is always sought.
Through frozen realms, we chase what's true,
With dreams adrift, and skies so blue.

Rhythms of Hoarfrost and Calm

Under pale skies, a hush descends,
Whispers of hoarfrost where nature bends.
Softly wrapped in a silver shroud,
The world pauses, gentle and proud.

Frost patterns trace on windows clear,
A delicate art, a masterpiece near.
With each breath, the air turns still,
Embracing moments time cannot fill.

Birds rustle softly, searching ground,
In search of warmth where hope is found.
Among the stillness, they take flight,
In rhythms of calm, pure delight.

Branches bow to the weight of ice,
Holding secrets, silent and nice.
In this beauty, life seems to pause,
Reflecting nature's gentle cause.

With every heartbeat, winter sings,
As the cold reveals the joy it brings.
In harmony, we find retreat,
In rhythms soft, where hearts repeat.

The Magic of the Winter Sun

The morning light breaks free,
Casting shadows long and bright.
A golden glow begins to dance,
Warming hearts with sheer delight.

Frosted branches glisten clear,
Whispers of the chill they share.
Nature breathes a frosty hymn,
In the crisp and radiant air.

Children laugh and play outside,
Building shapes of snowy fun.
Their cheeks a rosy hue so bright,
Underneath the winter sun.

The world transforms in gentle hues,
As snowflakes swirl and twirl around.
Each moment feels like magic here,
In the warmth that can be found.

So let us cherish winter's grace,
Embrace the joy the season brings.
For in the cold, there lies a spark,
A warmth that makes our spirit sing.

A Tapestry of Icicles

Hanging down from rooftops high,
They shimmer like the stars at night.
A tapestry of frozen dreams,
Glittering in purest light.

Each icicle a silent tale,
Of winter's harsh and gentle art.
A masterpiece of nature's hand,
Crafted with a frosty heart.

They drape from eaves, a crystal fringe,
A curtain of the icy throne.
Together they create a scene,
A world of magic, all their own.

Sunlight kisses every edge,
Creating prisms, bright and clear.
A wondrous sight in quiet chill,
Nature’s beauty, drawing near.

Underneath the winter’s breath,
We marvel at this frozen lace.
A fleeting gift from days gone by,
To hold, to cherish, in this place.

Breath of the Frosted Night

The moon hangs low, a silvery coin,
Casting spells upon the ground.
The air is crisp, the stars alight,
In winter's essence, peace is found.

A blanket forms of softest white,
Dreams unfold beneath the tree.
Whispers of the night, so calm,
Echoing through eternity.

Footprints crunch on frosty ground,
Marking paths of those who've tread.
With every breath, a cloud appears,
As nature sleeps, all tucked in bed.

Beneath the sky, so vast and wide,
We breathe the stillness of the night.
Wrapped in blankets, hearts entwined,
Finding warmth in pure delight.

The frost will fade, the dawn will rise,
Yet in this moment, time stands still.
The breath of night, a sweet embrace,
Leaving echoes our hearts will fill.

Glacial Dreams Beneath the Stars

The night is draped in glinting white,
Beneath the gaze of twinkling stars.
The world transformed in silken grace,
Whispers of winter's gentle scars.

Mountains stand with regal pride,
Adorned with layers, soft and bright.
Dreams drift through the frozen air,
In the stillness of the night.

Each flake tells a story pure,
Of journeys traveled, memories made.
In the silence, echoes call,
As memories begin to fade.

We close our eyes and feel the chill,
Letting dreams take flight on high.
With every breath, the world unfolds,
As glacial visions drift and sigh.

Together we will chase the night,
Hand in hand, beneath the skies.
For in the dance of dreams so bold,
Lies warmth that never says goodbye.

Glimmers in the Frosted Depths

In the hush of early dawn,
Soft whispers dance on snow.
Glimmers twinkle, frost has drawn,
A tapestry aglow.

Beneath the chill, secrets lie,
Wrapped in winter's grace.
The world holds its breath, a sigh,
In this frozen embrace.

Shadows play in silver light,
As echoes fade away.
Nature's canvas, pure and bright,
Awaits the break of day.

In the depths, dreams softly glow,
With each shimmering breath.
A journey where the heart may go,
Through whispers, life and death.

Glimmers spark the silent night,
With every step we take.
In the frost, there shines a light,
A promise we won't break.

Trails of White and Wonder

Footprints mark the path we tread,
Through drifts of soft, white snow.
Nature wakes, the world has spread,
A blanket pure below.

Branches heavy with the chill,
Adorned in sparkling lace.
A tranquil hush, the air is still,
In this serene, white space.

Laughter echoes, hearts in flight,
As sleds collide with glee.
Through trails of joy, we greet the night,
Underneath the frosty tree.

Each flake tells its tale anew,
In winter's gentle sway.
A dance of white, the world feels true,
Where dreams of gold replay.

In whispers soft, the stories spun,
Of youth and fleeting days.
Trails of wonder, laughter won,
Guide us through winter's maze.

Glistening Boughs Under Moonlight

Glistening boughs, pale and bright,
Underneath the moon’s soft gaze.
Each branch adorned, a gentle sight,
In winter's quiet phase.

Silhouettes in silver sheen,
Whispers of the starlit sky.
Nature's art, serene and clean,
As the world breathes a sigh.

Crystals hang like fragile dreams,
Suspended in the night.
Echoing soft midnight themes,
Embraced by pale twilight.

With every breeze, the branches sway,
In a timeless, graceful dance.
Beneath the moon, shadows play,
In this winter's trance.

Glistening boughs hold tales untold,
Of moments passed and lost.
In their embrace, the heart feels bold,
No matter what the cost.

Secrets Hidden in the Cold

Secrets lie in winter's fold,
Beneath the icy crust.
Stories whispered, faint and old,
Guarded by a shroud of dust.

Footsteps trace the paths of yore,
On the fields of frozen dreams.
Each breath a wish we can't ignore,
In silence, hope redeems.

The wind knows tales of past and gone,
With every chill it sends.
In the depths, a weary dawn,
Brings light where darkness bends.

Frosted air is thick with sighs,
Of lives that danced in glow.
In the cold where memory lies,
We find warmth in the snow.

Secrets hidden call us near,
In a gentle, soft embrace.
The winter’s song, a tune so clear,
Forever leaves its trace.

Silent Pines Whisper

In the stillness of the night,
Whispers softly take their flight.
Among the boughs where shadows play,
Pines speak secrets, come what may.

Moonlight dances on their skin,
Rustling leaves invite the din.
Gentle breezes weave a song,
Nature's chorus, deep and long.

Murmurs echo through the night,
Ancient tales brought to the light.
Every branch holds history,
Tales of life, of mystery.

Beneath the canopy so grand,
Where silence weaves a gentle strand.
Among the roots, a story grows,
Silent pines where wisdom flows.

Nestled in their calming shade,
Dreams and thoughts begin to wade.
In the heart of the dark wood,
Silent pines, forever good.

Frosted Twilight Trails

In the dusk where shadows blend,
Frosted paths around the bend.
Twilight glimmers on the trees,
Whispers carried by the breeze.

Gentle steps on icy ground,
Echo softly, peace profound.
Colors merge in dusky glow,
A world painted high and low.

Chill embraces every glance,
Nature's quiet, wistful dance.
Among the branches' silver lace,
Twilight trails, a tranquil space.

Moonlit vapors start to rise,
Stars awaken in the skies.
Every turn, a story told,
In this beauty, brave and bold.

Frosted whispers fill the air,
Magic sparkles everywhere.
As the night begins to fall,
Frosted trails enchant us all.

Shadows Beneath the Evergreens

In the depths where shadows lie,
Softly sighs the evening sky.
Evergreens stand tall and high,
Guardians of the night’s lullaby.

Silhouettes against the light,
Whisper secrets to the night.
Calm and cool, a gentle sigh,
Nature beckons, do not shy.

Footsteps traced through the dark,
Echos of a fading spark.
In the hush, a heartbeat sounds,
Life awakens, joy abounds.

Branches sway in soft ballet,
Tales of old that gently sway.
Beneath their watchful, loving gaze,
Shadows dance in twilight's haze.

Stillness falls, a sweet embrace,
In this sacred, quiet place.
Evergreens with arms held wide,
Shadows cradle, hearts confide.

Silence of the Sleeping Grove

In the quiet of the grove,
Nature rests, a peaceful trove.
Softly wrapped in evening's cloak,
Silence whispers, softly spoke.

Branches weave a gentle net,
Holding dreams we won’t forget.
Moonlight bathes the forest floor,
In this slumber, we explore.

Crickets sing a lullaby,
Underneath the starlit sky.
Every leaf and petal sways,
In the silence, beauty stays.

Nighttime breathes a soothing rhyme,
Cradles moments lost in time.
While the world is fast asleep,
In this grove, our hearts we keep.

Tucked away in nature’s arms,
Safe from life’s demanding charms.
Here beneath the ancient boughs,
Silence reigns, and peace allows.

The Cradle of Winter’s Stillness

In the hush of winter's breath,
Snowflakes dance on frozen streams.
The world is wrapped in white,
A lullaby of quiet dreams.

Trees stand tall, cloaked in light,
Branches bowed with icy grace.
Moonlight glimmers, soft and bright,
Painting shadows on this place.

Footprints trace a secret path,
Whispers echo, soft and low.
Nature's peace, a gentle bath,
In the cradle, time moves slow.

Every breath a frosty sigh,
As the night embraces all.
Stars above, a twinkling sky,
Winter's magic starts to call.

In this realm of purest white,
Silence sings a soothing tune.
Wrapped within the cloak of night,
Under the watch of the moon.

Nature's Crystal Fortress

Amidst the woods of frozen trees,
A fortress built of glistening frost.
Each branch adorned with crystal's ease,
In nature's realm, we count the cost.

Icicles hang like diamonds bright,
Reflecting light in a snowy haze.
Winter's breath, a pure delight,
In this fortress, time obeys.

Birds take flight on chilly air,
Their songs a call from heights above.
In this beauty, nothing's rare,
Nature cradles what we love.

Squirrels scurry, tails held high,
Searching for treasures left behind.
While the clouds drift in the sky,
Winter’s heart is ever kind.

Beneath the boughs, a world unfolds,
Whispers of life in frosty guise.
Nature's secrets gently told,
In this fortress, beauty lies.

A Symphony of Snow and Silence

As snowflakes fall, they softly play,
A melody of stillness, bright.
Each flake a note in winter's sway,
Composing dreams in soft twilight.

The world wrapped in a muted hue,
Nature's canvas, wide and deep.
In this silence, feelings brew,
While the stars above us keep.

Each breath we take, a cloud of white,
The hush of night, a calming sound.
In winter's grip, all feels so right,
On this magical, moonlit ground.

In whispers, trees embrace the chill,
Boughs adorned with snowy lace.
Nature's heart, so calm and still,
In this symphony, we find our place.

As darkness wraps the world in peace,
Melodies weave through every sigh.
A moment's pause, a sweet release,
In winter's arms, we fly high.

The Serenity of Enchanted Pines

In forests deep where pines do sway,
Serenity envelops all.
Their ancient whispers softly play,
In gentle winds, they rise and fall.

With needles green against the white,
A tapestry of nature's thread.
In stillness draped, a wondrous sight,
Underneath the sky widespread.

Crystals cling to every bough,
Nature's art, a stunning show.
In quiet moments, here and now,
The world transforms with every glow.

As shadows dance beneath the stars,
The pines stand watch, steadfast and true.
Guardians of dreams, near and far,
In their embrace, hope shines anew.

Beneath their watch, the soul finds peace,
In the magic that winter brings.
Where worries fade and joys increase,
Among the pines, the heart takes wings.

Frosted Whisperings

In the still of winter's breath,
Soft whispers dance on frozen air.
Leaves adorned with silver lace,
Nature sighs, free from despair.

Moonlight glints on frosted ground,
Echoes of the night resound.
Each flake a story, born of dreams,
A world transformed, or so it seems.

Branches droop beneath the weight,
Crystals gather, pure and bright.
The forest hushes, wrapped in peace,
A tranquil moment, time's release.

Beyond the woods, the stars align,
Whispers weave a stranger's tale.
In every glimmer, hope defined,
Frosted paths where spirits sail.

So linger in the chill of night,
Embrace the slumbering tones of deep.
For in the frost, there shines a light,
In whispered dreams, we quietly sleep.

Shadows Beneath the Pines

Beneath the pines, where shadows play,
The gentle rustle calls my name.
Whispers float on breezes gray,
Nature's secrets, wild and untamed.

Sunlight flickers through the boughs,
A dance of light on forest floor.
Each breeze a promise, soft as vows,
Beneath the trees, I long for more.

Mossy carpets cradle my feet,
Soft echoes of the past remain.
In solitude, I find retreat,
Within these woods, I feel no pain.

The scent of earth in twilight's glow,
A symphony of peace and grace.
In shadows deep, my spirit flows,
Lost in the beauty of this place.

So let the night engulf my soul,
For in this realm, I am alive.
With every sigh, I feel it whole,
Among the pines, my heart will thrive.

Echoes of Silent Snow

In the hush of falling flakes,
Echoes linger, soft and true.
Silent beauty, winter wakes,
A canvas painted fresh with hue.

Each crystal falls, a fleeting ghost,
Whispers wrapped in chilly air.
A quiet land, devoid of boast,
Nature's grace beyond compare.

Footsteps muted, hearts align,
With every pulse, a winter's thrill.
In this stillness, thoughts refine,
Amid the snow, we find our will.

Clouds drift low, a soft embrace,
Time grows still beneath the night.
In winter’s arms, we find our place,
Echoes whisper, pure delight.

So let the world in silence bloom,
For in this hush, love shines so bright.
In the echoes, dispel all gloom,
Together under stars, unite.

Crystals in the Canopy

Above the treetops, light refracts,
Crystals dangle, catching rays.
Nature’s art in fractured acts,
A prism's play in golden haze.

Branches sway with every breeze,
Whispers dance in vibrant hues.
Life explodes among the leaves,
A secret world with dreams to choose.

Glittering jewels in the high,
Nestled soft where silence flows.
In the green, where visions lie,
Crystals twinkle, ancient prose.

So let us wander, hearts in hand,
Underneath the swirling dance.
In this realm of wonderland,
Find our magic in the chance.

As sunlight fades to twilight's song,
Embrace the nights where stars ignite.
For in the canopy, we belong,
Crystals glitter, love's true light.

Frosted Heartbeats

In the chill of winter's breath,
Whispers dance on silent air.
Each heartbeat echoes softly,
In frost-kissed moments we share.

Snowflakes fall like gentle dreams,
Holding secrets of the night.
Beneath a blanket pure and white,
Love ignites with vibrant beams.

Candles flicker in the dark,
Casting shadows, soft and warm.
We find solace in the spark,
Embracing winter's frosty charm.

Time rewinds with each snowfall,
Memories wrapped in icy lace.
Our laughter echoes through it all,
A timeless, tender, warm embrace.

Hand in hand, we brave the cold,
Hearts entwined like ivy's climb.
In frosted glades, our love unfolds,
With every chill, we rise to prime.

The Icy Embrace of Time

Frozen moments linger still,
In the shadows of the past.
Whispers of a winter's thrill,
Echo where our hearts are cast.

Hours slide on silver streams,
Frosted memories softly glow.
In the silence of our dreams,
Time's cold touch begins to slow.

Seasons turn and spirits wane,
Yet we walk through crisp, still air.
In the quiet, love remains,
An icy ballad we both share.

Snowflakes swirl like fleeting hope,
In the tapestry of night.
With each breath, we learn to cope,
Finding warmth in chilly light.

Time may freeze, but hearts still beat,
In the woods where shadows play.
In each heartbeat, life’s sweet heat,
The icy grip fades away.

Secrets Laid Bare by Snow

Beneath the layers cold and white,
Secrets hide in winter's grace.
Whispers of a starry night,
Softly fall on nature's face.

Every flake a story told,
Memories wrapped in silence deep.
In the chill, our love unfolds,
While the world outside will sleep.

Echoes of a softer time,
Dance upon the snowy ground.
In the stillness, hearts entwine,
With each secret, warmth is found.

Past the frost, our truth lays bare,
In the quiet, dreams take flight.
Hope is woven with great care,
In the fabric of the night.

Snowflakes murmur, secrets shared,
In the glow of pale moon's gleam.
In the winter, hearts prepared,
For the warmth of love's pure dream.

The Call of the North Wind

Hear the whispers of the breeze,
As the north wind starts to sing.
Carrying tales through the trees,
Of ice and snow, a frosty spring.

With each gust, it stirs the soul,
Calling forth the dreams we chase.
In its chill, we find our goal,
Resilience wrapped in a warm embrace.

Across the hills where shadows lie,
Nature breathes a solemn hymn.
The north wind's voice will never die,
In its cry, we learn to swim.

We dance beneath the icy stars,
Following the wild call so clear.
With hope alive, we'll heal the scars,
In the brisk embrace, we steer.

Onward through the frosted night,
The north wind bears our courage high.
In its power, we find our light,
Together, we rise to the sky.

Lanterns of the Hoarfrost

In twilight's glow, the lanterns gleam,
Frosted whispers, a winter's dream.
Shadows dance on the icy ground,
Silent stories in silence found.

Beneath the stars, the world takes flight,
Each breath a cloud in the crisp night.
Lanterns flicker, warm and bright,
Guiding souls through frosted light.

Branches heavy with glistening ice,
Nature's jewels, so pure, so nice.
Each step a crunch, a love song clear,
Carried softly, the heart can hear.

With every glimmer, hope is spun,
A tapestry woven, day is done.
Embers of warmth in the chilly air,
Lanterns of hoarfrost, magic rare.

Together we wander, hand in hand,
In this winter's wonderland.
Where light and cold so deftly blend,
Our hearts, like lanterns, never end.

Dreaming Amongst the Fir

In the hush of pines, dreams take flight,
Whispers of wonder, cloaked in night.
Boughs sway gently in the breeze,
An invitation among the trees.

Mossy carpets, soft and green,
Draped in shadows, secrets unseen.
Stars peek through the needle's sway,
Guiding wanderers on their way.

Moonlight spills on the forest floor,
Painting tales of mythology and lore.
Each fir stands tall, a sentinel,
Guarding secrets it knows so well.

Under the canopy, spirits roam,
In the heart of the firs, we find our home.
Dreaming softly, the world retreats,
Lost in moments, our heartbeats meet.

Woven in dreams, our souls entwine,
In this sanctuary, pure and divine.
Amongst the fir, we find our grace,
In this sacred, enchanted space.

The Beauty of Bare Branches

Bare branches reach for the sky,
In the quiet stillness, time slips by.
Each twig a story, a whispered sigh,
In the heart of winter, dreams comply.

Framed against the soft twilight,
Silhouettes dance in fading light.
A testament to the seasons' flow,
In stark beauty, life starts to grow.

Laced with frost, they shimmer and shine,
Nature's art, so pure, so fine.
In their emptiness, a promise lies,
Of blossoms soon and azure skies.

Wind sings through the skeletal trees,
Carrying secrets on the breeze.
In their bare form, strength and grace,
A reminder that beauty finds its place.

Through every season, they stand so tall,
Bearing witness to the rise and fall.
In winter's grasp, we see their worth,
The beauty of bare branches, our earth.

Nightfall in the Frozen Hollow

As night descends in the frozen hollow,
Stars awaken, a silvered swallow.
Whispers of frost in the evening air,
Embrace the silence, a tranquil prayer.

Moonbeams drape like a gentle shawl,
Casting shadows that rise and fall.
Every whisper speaks of dreams,
In the stillness, imagination gleams.

Frozen grasses, crystal bright,
Reflect the glow of the moonlight.
In nature's pause, a breath we take,
Night's serenade, our hearts awake.

Across the expanse, the chill conceals,
Stories untold, the night reveals.
In the hollow's embrace, we find our peace,
In this frozen realm, troubles cease.

Wrapped in wonder, lost in trance,
Among the stars, we dare to dance.
Nightfall whispers its soothing call,
In the frozen hollow, we're free for all.

Moonlit Trails through Frozen Groves

Beneath the silver gleam so bright,
The trails weave softly through the night.
Whispers of wind in shadows dance,
In frozen silence, lost in trance.

Pine trees bowed under winter's weight,
Crystals sparkle, nature's fate.
Footsteps crunch on snow so deep,
Embracing secrets that woods keep.

Stars above in velvet skies,
Guide the wanderer with their sighs.
Each breath is sharp, the world aglow,
In moonlit trails where dreams can flow.

Frosted branches reach for space,
Nature's beauty, a tender embrace.
A path through wonder, cold yet warm,
In frozen groves, there's magic born.

As shadows dance in crystal air,
The heart beats wild, free from care.
A journey where the soul takes flight,
On moonlit trails, a sweet delight.

The Breath of an Icy Night

The breath of night, so cold and clear,
Wraps the world that we hold dear.
Stars twinkle like ice in the sky,
A hush descends as time slips by.

Frosted fields in silent repose,
Nature's artistry, soft as a rose.
Chill air fills lungs with a tranquil peace,
In icy stillness, worries cease.

Moonbeams weave through branches bare,
Casting shadows with utmost care.
Echoes of night serenade the dark,
In the heart's silence, a magical spark.

Each breath taken in the shivering light,
An invitation to bask in the night.
Where thoughts can wander, free of fright,
In the breath of an icy night.

Moments drift like snowflakes bold,
In the gentle caress of the cold.
Frozen whispers wrap around,
In every silence, beauty found.

A Stillness Among the Trees

In the stillness deep, where shadows play,
Among the trees, I drift away.
Whispers of leaves in a gentle sway,
Nature's lullaby at the close of day.

Branches intertwine, an ancient song,
A refuge where the heart belongs.
Every silence holds a tale,
In the embrace of trees, I sail.

Frost blankets softly on bark and ground,
A tranquil beauty that knows no bounds.
The quiet hum of life surrounds,
In stillness, the sacred resounds.

Time slows down in the evening light,
A canvas painted with stars so bright.
Every breath a gift from the trees,
In their presence, I find my ease.

Nature’s heart beats in every nook,
In harmony, I take my look.
A stillness that whispers and sings,
Among the trees, my spirit takes wings.

Frost-Kissed Dreams

In twilight's glow, the air turns crisp,
Whispering secrets in nature's lisp.
Frost-kissed dreams drift in the night,
Painting visions with silver light.

Each flake a promise, delicate, rare,
Caught in the dance of the cold night air.
With every breath, hope takes its flight,
In the tender grip of stars so bright.

The world transformed, a frozen muse,
Every shadow a magic fuse.
With dreams wrapped tight in winter's shroud,
The heart beats loud, adept and proud.

Moments linger, enshrouded in peace,
While frosty wonders never cease.
A celestial canvas where thoughts can dream,
In the still of night, a quiet stream.

Frost-kissed whispers on the lips of dawn,
As night retreats, the magic drawn.
Cherished moments, soon to awake,
In the dawn's embrace, new paths we take.

Beneath the Frosty Canopy

Underneath the icicle shade,
Whispers of winter softly played.
Branches draped in crystal white,
A silent dance, a cold delight.

The ground enveloped in a shroud,
Nature keeps her secrets loud.
Footsteps muffled, silence deep,
In frosty dreams, the world does sleep.

Frosted leaves like diamonds shine,
Each breath visible, pure and fine.
A realm where time is paused in breath,
Beneath the trees, a hush of death.

Through the branches, shadows creep,
Guardians of the secrets keep.
In this tranquil, frigid space,
Life's gentle pulse, a fleeting trace.

The moonlight casts its silver glow,
Illuminates the world below.
In the stillness where hearts align,
Beneath the frost, we intertwine.

Fragments of Ice and Time

Scattered crystals on the ground,
Whispers of a past profound.
Moments captured, frozen tight,
Fragments glinting in moonlight.

Echoes linger on the breeze,
Time suspended, as it frees.
Mirrors of our yesterdays,
In the ice, their spirit stays.

Each shard a memory, sharp and bright,
Glinting softly in the night.
Through each corner, shadows play,
Fragments gather, drift away.

Yet in stillness, lessons freeze,
Understanding, like the trees.
Winter's breath, a quiet rhyme,
In the struggles of our time.

Let the ice remind us well,
In each story, secrets dwell.
For as the seasons come and go,
Life unfolds through ice and snow.

The Schema of Shadows in Chill

Shadows stretch in evening's glow,
Crafted lines in silver snow.
Chill descends with silent grace,
In the dark, we find our place.

Shapes emerge from twilight's hold,
Stories of the brave and bold.
Every corner wrapped in night,
The shadows dance, a waltz of light.

Echoes whisper, softly tread,
In the chill where dreams are bred.
Each outline tells a tale untold,
Of warmth enduring through the cold.

Night unfolds its cloak so wide,
Inside its depths, we must confide.
With every breath, shadows sway,
Writing maps, they guide our way.

Beneath the stars, a quiet thrill,
The schema of our hearts does fill.
In the chill where silence reigns,
Life repeats, despite the pains.

Epiphanies in the White Silence

In silence deep, truths unfold,
The whispers of winter, stories told.
Snowflakes dance in soft embrace,
Muffled thoughts in a tranquil space.

Frozen breath hangs in the air,
Epiphanies born from moments rare.
Each flake a dream, each drift a clue,
In the white silence, I find what's true.

The world slows down, a gentle sigh,
In stillness, we learn how to fly.
Nature speaks in the softest tone,
In the quiet, we're never alone.

Footprints trace a story near,
Echoes whisper, drawing us near.
With every flake, wisdom grows shy,
In the white silence, I learn to try.

Here in the hush, we come alive,
In the beauty of calm, we can thrive.
Voices merge in the quiet night,
Epiphanies whisper, hearts take flight.

Voices of the Subdued Earth

Beneath the snow, the earth holds dreams,
Whispers soft in the flowing streams.
Roots tangled deep, a secret song,
In silence, life beats strong.

The stones speak truths long forgotten,
Where shadows dance in the sunken cotton.
Echos of laughter, memories stirred,
In the subdued earth, no voice unheard.

Each breath of wind, a tender sigh,
Connects us to where the past lies.
Slowly, gently, the stories rise,
From buried hopes to the expansive skies.

Listen close to what's beneath,
The sighs of soil, the rhythm of breath.
In the quiet, we learn to see,
The voices speak, they set us free.

To honor the past, we must explore,
The wisdom hidden deep in the core.
Embrace the earth, rich and profound,
In the subdued, life's beauty is found.

Reflections in an Icy Stream

Mirrored stillness, water so clear,
I see my thoughts, my heart sincere.
Ripples echo, life flows by,
In icy reflections, I learn to fly.

Fleeting moments caught in time,
Each glance a word, a subtle rhyme.
Nature’s canvas, silent and bright,
In the stream's depths, shadows ignite.

The chill awakens what lies inside,
Emotions dance like leaves in the tide.
A glimpse of hope in each gentle sway,
In the icy stream, I find my way.

Footsteps pause at the water’s edge,
Life unfolds in a whispered pledge.
A promise wrapped in winter's gleam,
In reflections, I chase the dream.

Time stands still, worries cease,
In the icy stream, I find my peace.
Flowing softly, wisdom streams,
Reflections whisper of my dreams.

A Memoir of Snow-Draped Pines

Tall sentinels dressed in white,
Guardians of dreams, veiled in light.
Beneath their boughs, warm secrets hide,
In the snow's embrace, we glide.

Branches sway with stories told,
Of winter nights and adventures bold.
Each flake a memory, soft and bright,
A memoir woven in the moon's light.

Whispers of the forest, soft and low,
In the pines, time starts to flow.
Echoes of laughter blend with the chill,
In nature's embrace, hearts grow still.

Silhouettes dance in twilight's glow,
Underneath the stars, where dreams flow.
The pines hold witness to the night,
In this memoir, everything feels right.

So let us wander, let us roam,
In the arms of the pines, we find our home.
A tapestry woven in white and green,
In the snow-draped pines, our souls convene.

The Calm Before the Thaw

In the hush before the dawn,
Snowflakes float, a gentle fawn.
The air is still, the world holds breath,
Awaiting spring to conquer death.

Trees stand tall in silver pride,
Wrapped in frost, their arms open wide.
A promise whispers in the breeze,
The thaw will come to wake the leaves.

Rivers sleep beneath a veil,
Silent echoes of nature's tale.
Each second drips like melting ice,
A quiet moment, pure and nice.

Soon the sun will cast its rays,
And melt away the cold gray haze.
With vibrant blooms, the earth will sing,
From winter's chill, we'll see the spring.

So in this pause, we find our peace,
A gentle time, a sweet release.
We gather hope as shadows fade,
In beauty's arms, we will wade.

Echoes of Whispering Winds

High above, the soft winds sigh,
Carrying tales from earth to sky.
Whispers weave through branches bare,
Secrets dance in crisp, cool air.

Through the pines, a story flows,
Of distant lands where sunlight glows.
Each gust a poem, wild and free,
Singing softly, just for me.

Clouds gather like a drifting thought,
In their shadows, warmth is sought.
Echoes fade, yet linger still,
The winds remind us of our will.

A gentle sigh, a haunting breeze,
Through barren fields and frosted trees.
Nature's voice, a timeless song,
Guides our hearts where we belong.

So let us listen, hearts awake,
To the secrets that the breezes take.
For in each whisper, truth is found,
In echoes soft, the world’s profound.

Twilight's Embrace on Frosted Ground

Twilight falls on a silver scene,
Each breath a puff, a gentle sheen.
Stars awaken in the night sky,
Whispering dreams as they drift by.

Frosted grass beneath our feet,
Nature's hush, so calm and sweet.
The moonlight spills like melted gold,
Stories shared and dreams foretold.

Shadows stretch as daylight fades,
Bringing forth the night's cascades.
A blanket of stars, crisp and bright,
Cradling the world in soft twilight.

Whispers linger in the cold air,
Magic dances everywhere.
In this moment, all is still,
The heart finds rest, the soul can feel.

Embrace the night, let worries cease,
In twilight's arms, we find our peace.
For when the sun begins to rise,
We'll carry these dreams to the skies.

Murmurs Beneath the Cold Sky

Beneath the vast and frozen dome,
Whispers linger, far from home.
Each murmur stirs the silent night,
Hidden tales, out of sight.

In the stillness, secrets call,
Frosted breath, a mystic thrall.
Nature speaks, though lips don't part,
Echoing softly in the heart.

Softly glows the distant star,
Guiding wanderers from afar.
Through the chill, a warmth ignites,
Hope is born in starry nights.

As the cold wraps round the ground,
Still there's beauty to be found.
In every breath, a promise stays,
To lead us through the darkest days.

So listen close to what's unsaid,
For in the silence, love is spread.
Murmurs weave a soft disguise,
Beneath the blanket of the skies.

Dreamscapes of a Frigid Realm

In twilight's grasp, the cold winds sigh,
Whispers of frost where shadows lie.
A moonlit glow on icy streams,
Awakens thoughts, ignites our dreams.

Crystals dance upon the trees,
Each breath a cloud in winter's freeze.
Beneath the stars, the silence grows,
As night unfolds, a beauty flows.

Footprints lead on paths of white,
Guided by the silver light.
In frozen realms where echoes fade,
A world awaits, adventures laid.

Glistening fields, untouched and pure,
A magic realm we can't ignore.
In dreamscapes vast, we can be free,
In frigid lands of mystery.

Hearts that thrum in frozen air,
Find solace in the stillness there.
Amidst the chill, we find our way,
Through winter's song, we choose to stay.

The Quietude After the Storm

The tempest roared, it shook the night,
Now dawn breaks soft, with gentle light.
A hush envelops, sweet and clear,
As nature sighs, we draw so near.

Raindrops glisten on the ground,
The world reborn, with peace unbound.
Leaves weave stories, fresh and bright,
In tranquil whispers, life takes flight.

Birds return with melodies sweet,
Syncing hearts to a steady beat.
In the stillness, hope takes root,
From chaos born, the calm is fruit.

Paths once muddy, now anew,
Painted skies in a vibrant hue.
Each breath we take, a gift, a sign,
From storm to calm, the stars align.

With every step, we feel the grace,
Of nature's hand, in this sacred space.
Together we rise, from scars that heal,
In quietude, our hearts can feel.

Shards of Crystal in the Forest

Amongst the pines, where shadows play,
Glistening shards bring light to gray.
A silent beauty, pure and bright,
Reflects the sun in joyous flight.

Each crystal formed, a tale untold,
Of ancient whispers, brave and bold.
Through dappled light, the colors beam,
In woodland realms, they weave a dream.

Footsteps soft on carpeted ground,
In nature’s cradle, peace is found.
The forest breathes, a living hymn,
Where shards of crystal deeply brim.

Echoes of laughter softly soar,
As magic lingers, evermore.
A shimmered path, our hearts align,
In nature's grasp, we find the divine.

From hidden depths, the gems arise,
A breathtaking gift beneath blue skies.
In every shard, a world to see,
In crystal light, we are set free.

A Solstice Serenade

Beneath the stars, the night so clear,
We gather close, in warmth and cheer.
With whispered songs the fire glows,
As voices dance in twinkling rows.

The solstice brings a timeless grace,
We celebrate in this sacred space.
A cycle turns, the year's embrace,
As dreams collide, in twilight's chase.

With every note, a story spun,
Of changing seasons, joys begun.
In harmony, we find our way,
Through fleeting night and dawning day.

The ancient tale of light reborn,
A promise made with each new morn.
As shadows fade, we rise anew,
In festive hearts, the light breaks through.

With dancing flames, we raise our voice,
In every heart, a whispered choice.
To cherish moments, near or far,
In this serenade, our guiding star.

Echoes in the Icy Vale

In the vale where silence reigns,
Whispers dance on frozen chains.
Frosty breath in twilight's glow,
Echoes linger, soft and slow.

Beneath the sky, so still, so wide,
Nature's secrets softly bide.
Amid the trees, shadows play,
Night unfolds, the end of day.

Footsteps crunch on icy ground,
Each sound in stillness drowned.
A memory, faint yet clear,
In this vale, all is near.

Stars emerge in velvet hue,
Glowing softly, dream-like view.
Underneath the watchful night,
Echoes fade to softest light.

With every breath, the chill surrounds,
In the vale, the heart resounds.
Winter's grip both sweet and dire,
Stories told by hearts afire.

Hushed Footsteps on Snow

In the stillness, footsteps tread,
A trail of whispers, softly spread.
Snowflakes fall in gentle grace,
Draping all in a white embrace.

Each crunch beneath the weight of night,
A testament to quiet light.
Hushed echoes in the frosty air,
Nature's lullaby everywhere.

Through the woods, a path unfolds,
Stories hidden, long since told.
The moonlight casts a silver sheen,
A peaceful world, serene, unseen.

Branches bend with heavy loads,
Marking soft and winding roads.
A journey silent, whispers blend,
Where every step feels like a friend.

In this calm, where spirits soar,
Footsteps pause, forevermore.
Embracing winter's gentle hold,
In hushed stories, pure and bold.

Embrace of the Brisk Breeze

Through the trees, a brisk wind weaves,
Carrying tales of fallen leaves.
A breath of chill, a sweet caress,
Nature’s song in its best dress.

With every gust, the branches sway,
Dancing softly, night and day.
Whispers call from hills afar,
Tales of longing, dreams, and stars.

Beckoning hearts to wander free,
In the dance of the wild spree.
The cool embrace ignites the soul,
A moment still, a fleeting goal.

Through the vale, the secrets flow,
In the softest ebb and flow.
With open arms, I welcome night,
Embraced by whispers, pure delight.

In every sigh of nature's breath,
Lives the echo of battle's death.
Yet here, among the swaying trees,
We find our home in tender breeze.

A Shiver Beneath the Twigs

Underneath the brittle twigs,
Where shadows dance, the cold heart digs.
A shiver stirs, a breath of frost,
In quiet woods, no echo lost.

Each crackle underfoot invites,
The silent charm of winter nights.
Pine-scented air, crisp and bright,
Wraps the world in muted light.

Beneath the moon's soft, watchful eye,
The whispered secrets flutter by.
A rhythm born from night’s embrace,
In shadows deep, we find our place.

Echoes linger in the pines,
Each rustling leaf, a tale that shines.
Through barren limbs and frost-kissed air,
A symphony beyond compare.

So hold the stillness, cherish grace,
In nature's heart, we find our space.
With every shiver, under twigs,
A bond unfolds, as the night digs.

Mysteries Beneath the Icicles

Beneath the hang of frozen tears,
Secrets whisper, lost and near.
Shadows dance in the pale moonlight,
Veils of frost obscure the sight.

Ancient stories trapped in glass,
Echoes of the seasons pass.
A world of silence, deep and cold,
Hidden wonders yet untold.

Icicles guard their crystal keep,
Where winter's secrets quietly sleep.
Each drip a note in nature's song,
A symphony where dreams belong.

In the heart of winter's breath,
Lies the beauty born of death.
Fragile blooms in icy lands,
Nature's art from frozen hands.

Beneath the chill, the pulse runs strong,
In the quiet, we all belong.
Mysteries beckon, bright and bold,
In the winter, life unfolds.

Sledge Trails in Wild Whimsy

Through valleys deep where laughter swells,
Sledge trails weave their playful spells.
Tiny footprints mark the way,
In the gleam of winter's play.

Over hills of sparkling white,
Joyous echoes take to flight.
Children shout, their spirits free,
Riding waves of jubilee.

Frosty breaths in the morning air,
Moments captured, wild and rare.
Slides of wonder, gentle leaps,
In the heart where childhood keeps.

Winding paths where stories grow,
Snowflakes dance in a twirling show.
With every turn, pure delight,
We chase the magic of the night.

And as the sun dips low in sky,
Dreams drift softly, sweet and spry.
In whirls of laughter, we rejoice,
Sledge trails hum our vibrant voice.

The Comfort of Cold

In the hush of falling snow,
Winter wraps the world in glow.
Breath of frost upon the skin,
A gentle peace, where warmth begins.

Pines stand tall in white embrace,
Winter's charm, a sacred space.
Each flake a kiss from skies above,
Crisp and clear, the air we love.

Fires crackle, embers hum,
Comfort finds its way to come.
Blankets pull us close and tight,
In the calm of winter's night.

Through the window, soft and serene,
A canvas pure, a tranquil scene.
Nature whispers, deep and slow,
In the heart, a warm glow.

Embrace the chill, let spirits rise,
In quiet moments, truth lies.
With every breath, we slowly fold,
Finding solace in the cold.

A Frosty Overture among the Trees

In the forest where silence reigns,
Frosty whispers weave through the chains.
Branches bow with a heavy dress,
Nature hums in timelessness.

Silver sparkles in the dawn's light,
A frosty overture takes flight.
Leaves like crystals, bright and rare,
Intricate beauty hung in air.

Footsteps crunch on snow-clad ground,
In winter's hand, magic is found.
Each breath a plume in the stillness,
In the heart, a quiet thrillness.

Timber's sigh encased in ice,
A tranquil world, so pure, so nice.
Sculpted forms in the morning's glow,
A frosted path where wonders flow.

Among the trees, the spirits dance,
In this realm, we find our chance.
To breathe the air that nature gives,
In frosty dreams, forever lives.

A Symphony of Frostbite

In the stillness of the night,
I hear the crisp air play,
Notes of icy whispers,
Dancing in moonlight's sway.

Crystal shards on branches,
Glisten like tiny gems,
Nature's soft embrace,
In winter's frozen hymn.

Snowflakes twirl and flutter,
Painting the earth with grace,
A melody of silence,
In this enchanted place.

Echoes of the frost,
Chanting their gentle tune,
Each breath of winter air,
Underneath the pale moon.

As the dawn breaks slowly,
The symphony begins to fade,
Yet in my heart I hold,
This magic that was made.

The Beauty of a Silent Thaw

In the hush of morning light,
Whispers of warmth unfold,
Melting ice begins to sing,
Stories of spring retold.

Rivers break their winter chains,
Flowing free once more,
Each drop a note of joy,
As they kiss the shore.

Bud and bloom awaken,
Filling the air with scents,
Life bursts forth from slumber,
Nature's sweet recompense.

Soft rains invite the earth,
To shed its chilly skin,
In the beauty of a thaw,
New beginnings begin.

With every gentle murmur,
Life's promise starts to play,
In the silence of the thaw,
Hope gives birth to day.

When the Earth Holds Its Breath

Silent pause in twilight's glow,
As if time has ceased to flow,
The world wrapped in a quiet shroud,
Underneath the starry crowd.

Snowflakes settle, soft and light,
Each one a story, a fleeting sight,
Crystals twinkle in dark night's keep,
While the earth lies fast asleep.

The moon casts shadows, cool and pale,
Whispers drift in the frosty gale,
In the stillness, secrets lie,
As the world holds a breath, a sigh.

Frozen streams reflect the skies,
Nature's canvas, where beauty lies,
With every heartbeat, a silent pledge,
In the earth's stillness, we find the edge.

Then as dawn begins to break,
Life stirs softly, a gentle shake,
When the earth exhales its dreams,
Awakening with golden beams.

Whispers of Cold Fragrance

In the air, a chill so sweet,
Fragrant hints of winter's greet,
Pine and cedar, scents so bold,
In the silence, stories told.

Frosted breath upon the trees,
Mingling with the whispering breeze,
Each moment a scented note,
On the frost, like petals float.

Icicles hanging, sharp and clear,
Nature's art, both strange and dear,
A fragrance held in frozen time,
Like poetry, it begins to rhyme.

Every corner holds a tale,
Of crisp adventures, brisk and pale,
With each scent, memories dance,
In winter's deep, a fleeting glance.

So let us breathe this air so bright,
In the realm of cold and light,
For in these whispers, we will find,
The beauty of the frozen kind.

A Canvas of Evergreens and Snowdrifts

In the hush of winter's night,
Evergreens stand tall and bright.
Snowdrifts cover, pure as lace,
Nature's artwork, a serene embrace.

Whispers echo through the trees,
Carried softly by the breeze.
Each branch holds a crystal crown,
In this silent, snowy town.

Footprints mark a secret trail,
Where dreams of winter softly sail.
Children laugh and spirits fly,
Beneath the vast, unyielding sky.

As twilight weaves its silver thread,
Stars awaken overhead.
The canvas stretches, wide and free,
A masterpiece for all to see.

Glimmers dance on icy streams,
Reflecting softly all our dreams.
A world wrapped in soft white glow,
In this canvas of ebb and flow.

Frost's Gentle Caress on Boughs

Frost creeps gently on the pines,
Shimmering like delicate lines.
Boughs bow low with silver weight,
Nature's touch, so light and great.

Morning breaks with golden light,
Frosty breath gives pause to flight.
Each twig glimmers, a fleeting sight,
Transforming woods from dark to bright.

Whispers of the winter's song,
In this realm, where we belong.
Beneath a quilt of icy sheen,
Every moment, pure and clean.

Pattering of tiny feet,
Nature’s lullaby, soft beat.
In the stillness, hearts are found,
Loss and peace in balance, bound.

As day fades into twilight's arms,
Frosty beauty, nature's charms.
In quiet awe, we stand bemused,
By the spell that frost infused.

Where Night Meets Ice

Where night meets ice, a dance unfolds,
Moonlight kisses, the world beholds.
Stars twinkle on a frozen sea,
A realm of magic, wild and free.

Crisp air tinged with dreams untold,
Whispers of secrets, bright and bold.
Every shadow a haunting sigh,
As the northern lights paint the sky.

Silent echoes of gentle breath,
Nature's hush, embracing death.
In the stillness, a moment's grace,
In the quiet, we find our place.

Crystal branches bend and sway,
In the seduction of the fray.
Fingers of frost trace the land,
In this fragile, frozen band.

Where night meets ice, we are alive,
In the cold, our spirits thrive.
Together, we share this blissful night,
Under the spells of soft moonlight.

Sentinels of the Frozen Hollow

Tall sentinels guard the hollow,
With branches laden, a timeless bough.
In the heart of winter’s reign,
Whispers echo, sweet but plain.

Shadows dance and softly sway,
In the fading light of day.
Each flake fluttering from the sky,
Kisses softly as they lie.

A kingdom draped in softest white,
Beneath a blanket, pure and right.
Silent watches, night descends,
In the frozen realm, where magic blends.

From the boughs, the frost does drip,
Each drop a tale of winter's trip.
In the hollow, secrets bloom,
In this still and silent room.

Sentinels keep their watchful gaze,
Through the nights and endless days.
In their care, we dream and roam,
Finding warmth in this icy home.

Sled Tracks in the December Silence

The morning hush, a blanket white,
Sled tracks carve the snow, pure delight.
Echoes of laughter ride the breeze,
In the heart of winter, joy's sweet freeze.

Pine trees bow under the heavy load,
Whispers of frost on the winding road.
Children's faces aglow with cheer,
As winter's magic draws them near.

The sun peeks out, a gentle light,
Glowing softly, warming the night.
Each slide down brings a joyful shout,
In December's wonder, there is no doubt.

Clouds drift slowly, painting the skies,
A soft reflection as daylight flies.
Sled tracks vanish, but joy remains,
In the silence, sweet memory reigns.

With twilight falling, the world aglow,
Night wraps the earth in a velvet throw.
The magic lingers in snowy ground,
In every heartbeat, winter is found.

Beneath the Weight of Winter's Embrace

The world transformed, a crystal glow,
Beneath the weight of soft, white snow.
Branches sag under their crystal crown,
In winter’s grip, the silence drowns.

Footprints lead to sanctuary warm,
Life sheltered from the raging storm.
Inside, the fire crackles with cheer,
While outside cold whispers secrets near.

Each breath released, a cloud of mist,
Nature's beauty begs to be kissed.
Frozen streams with a glassy sheen,
Reflecting all that once had been.

Stars flicker through the velvet night,
Each one a promise of morning light.
Hope lingers in the frostbitten air,
Beneath winter’s weight, we find our care.

Embraced by the chill, yet hearts feel warm,
In the stillness, we weather the storm.
Together we stand, hand in hand,
Bound by love in this frozen land.

Flakes that Paint the Evergreen

Falling softly, delicate grace,
Flakes that dance, a gentle embrace.
They blanket the earth, a soft white quilt,
Painting the world, where winter is built.

Pine trees stand tall, cloaked in white,
Each bough adorned, a wondrous sight.
Snowflakes twirl in the crisp, cool air,
Nature’s artwork, beyond compare.

Glistening jewels on branches sway,
As whispered secrets in silence play.
Nature’s brush strokes, so serene,
Creating a canvas, alive, pristine.

With every flake, a story is spun,
Of winter's magic, of cold and sun.
The world transformed, a fairy tale,
In the forest's depths, where wonders prevail.

As night descends, the moon peeks through,
Casting shadows in the tranquil dew.
Flakes that paint the evergreen stay,
In our hearts, they melt away.

Echoes of Nature's Slumber

In winter’s hush, all seems at rest,
Echoes of nature, a silent fest.
The woods lie still, a peaceful sight,
Wrapped in dreams, cloaked in white.

Animals hide in their cozy dens,
While snow drapes softly, the earth it lends.
A world at rest, beneath the moon,
Cradled gently, to winter’s tune.

Frosted fields, a gentle sigh,
Whispers of life drifting softly by.
Stars commentate in twinkling tones,
A symphony played among the stones.

In the stillness, time holds its breath,
Each moment cherished, life and death.
The beauty found in quiet grace,
In winter’s arms, we find our place.

Echoes linger, a tender sound,
Nature's lullaby stands profound.
As spring awaits the thawing heat,
We cherish stillness, and savor the sweet.

www.ingramcontent.com/pod-product-compliance
Ingram Content Group UK Ltd.
Pitfield, Milton Keynes, MK11 3LW, UK
UKHW031944151224
452382UK00006B/125

9 789908 520087